OUT OF THIS WORLD

SPACE TRAVEL

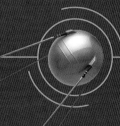

AARON DEYOE

Consulting Editor, Diane Craig, M.A./Reading Specialist

Super Sandcastle

An Imprint of Abdo Publishing
abdopublishing.com

ABDOPUBLISHING.COM

Published by Abdo Publishing, a division of ABDO, PO Box 398166, Minneapolis, Minnesota 55439. Copyright © 2016 by Abdo Consulting Group, Inc. International copyrights reserved in all countries. No part of this book may be reproduced in any form without written permission from the publisher. Super SandCastle™ is a trademark and logo of Abdo Publishing.

Printed in the United States of America, North Mankato, Minnesota
062015
092015

THIS BOOK CONTAINS RECYCLED MATERIALS

Editor: Liz Salzmann
Content Developer: Nancy Tuminelly
Cover and Interior Design and Production: Mighty Media, Inc.
Photo Credits: NASA, ESA, Shutterstock

Library of Congress Cataloging-in-Publication Data

DeYoe, Aaron, author.
  Space travel / Aaron DeYoe ; consulting editor, Diane Craig, M.A./Reading Specialist.
    pages cm. -- (Out of this world)
  Audience: K to grade 4.
  ISBN 978-1-62403-745-0
1. Space flight--Juvenile literature. 2. Space vehicles--Juvenile literature. 3. Interplanetary voyages--Juvenile literature. I. Title.
  TL793.D473 2016
  629.45--dc23
                              2015002060

Super SandCastle™ books are created by a team of professional educators, reading specialists, and content developers around five essential components—phonemic awareness, phonics, vocabulary, text comprehension, and fluency—to assist young readers as they develop reading skills and strategies and increase their general knowledge. All books are written, reviewed, and leveled for guided reading, early reading intervention, and Accelerated Reader™ programs for use in shared, guided, and independent reading and writing activities to support a balanced approach to literacy instruction.

CONTENTS

SPACE TRAVEL

PEOPLE USED TO DREAM of going into space. But they didn't know how. Today we have many ways to explore space.

Rockets can bring people to other worlds.

Space probes study faraway planets.

Rovers can drive on planets and moons.

VISIONS OF SPACE

Ancient people watched the stars. They wanted to try space travel. Some thought a big balloon would work. Others thought a cannon would work.

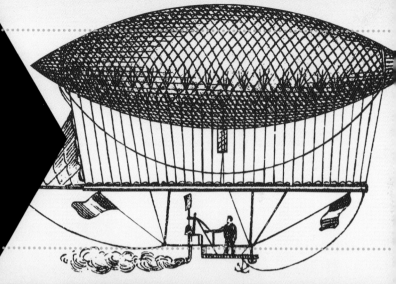

ROCKET CHAIR

Wan Hu was a Chinese scientist. He lived in the 1500s. He tried to travel into space. He filled 47 rockets with **gunpowder**. He tied them to a chair. He sat in the chair. His servants lit the rockets. Wan Hu was never seen again.

MAKE IT GO!

ROCKET ENGINES

An explosion happens at one end of a rocket. The explosion pushes it into space.

ION THRUSTER

An ion thruster shoots beams of atoms backward. This makes the spacecraft go forward.

THERE ARE MANY WAYS TO MOVE IN SPACE.

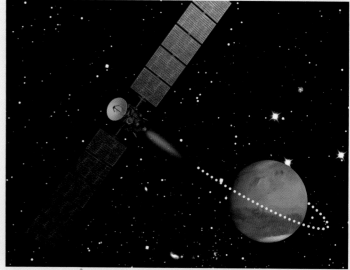

SOLAR SAIL

A solar sail uses energy from the sun. The energy gets caught in the sails. This moves the spacecraft forward.

GRAVITY ASSIST

Sometimes a spacecraft flies near a planet. The planet's gravity throws the spacecraft. This helps save fuel.

EARLY TRAVEL

People have been sending things into space since 1942.

Germany sent the first rocket into space. It was in 1942.

Sputnik was the first object to orbit Earth. The Soviet Union sent it in 1957.

The first man went into space in 1961. His name was Yuri Gagarin. His spacecraft orbited Earth once.

SATURN V ROCKET

SATURN V ROCKETS took people to the moon. The United States sent 13 of them. They were used from 1967 to 1973.

← LUNAR MODULE

The rocket had many parts. The top held the lunar module. The lunar module landed on the moon.

GIRAFFE

18 feet
(5.5 m)

STATUE OF LIBERTY

151 feet
(46 m)

SPACE SHUTTLE

184.2 feet
(56.1 m)

BIG BEN

315.9 feet
(96.3 m)

SATURN V ROCKET

363 feet
(110.6 m)

EXTERNAL TANK

SOLID ROCKET BOOSTER

ORBITER

CARGO BAY

SPACE SHUTTLE

THE SPACE SHUTTLES were reusable. Rockets lifted an orbiter into space. Then the rockets fell off. The orbiter carried astronauts around the Earth. Then it came back to Earth. It landed on a **runway**.

ALL-PURPOSE

The space shuttles had many jobs. They helped send satellites into space. They brought scientists to fix satellites. They took people to the International Space Station. They were also used as science labs.

END OF THE SHUTTLES

There were 135 space shuttle **missions**. The first was in 1981. The last was in 2011. NASA is working on newer rockets.

SATELLITES

A **SATELLITE** orbits another object in space. The moon is a satellite of Earth. There are also man-made satellites. People send them into space.

EARTH SATELLITES

Satellites near Earth do many things. Some help with radio and TV connections. Others help with maps and directions. Scientists use others to study the weather.

SATELLITES IN USE

HUBBLE SPACE TELESCOPE

The *Hubble Space Telescope* orbits Earth. It takes pictures of space.

VENUS EXPRESS

Venus Express orbits Venus. The European Space Agency built it. It studies the air around Venus.

MARS RECONNAISSANCE ORBITER (MRO)

The MRO orbits Mars. It makes maps of Mars.

SPACE PROBES

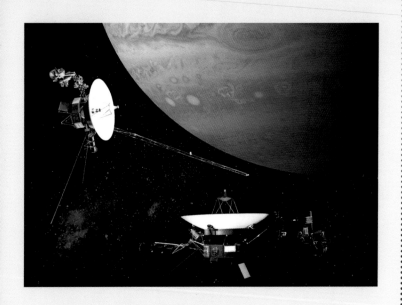

VOYAGER 1 AND 2

Voyager 1 and 2 visited the outer planets.
Voyager 1 even left our solar system. It was
the first probe to do so.

KEPLER

Kepler is a space telescope. It looks for
planets orbiting other stars. It has found
more than a thousand planets!

SPACE PROBES are a type of spacecraft. They study many things in space. They can orbit planets and moons. They can even follow **comets**!

STARDUST

Stardust was spacecraft that studied comets. It collected dust from a comet's tail. It brought the dust back to Earth.

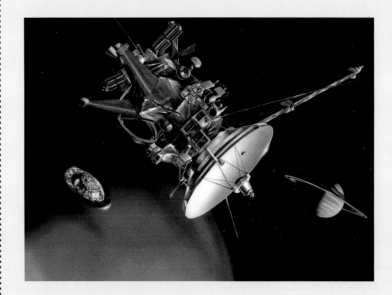

CASSINI-HUYGENS

Cassini-Huygens studies Jupiter and Saturn. It takes pictures of the planets and their moons.

LANDERS

LUNA 9

The Soviet Union sent *Luna 9* to the moon. It landed there in 1966.

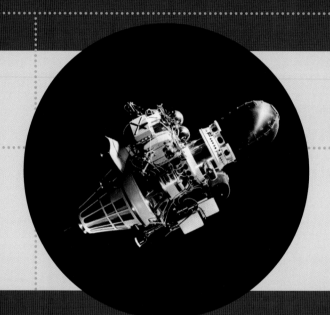

LUNAR MODULE

The lunar module was part of the Saturn V rocket. It took people to the moon's surface. The top part could lift off. It came back to Earth.

CASSINI-HUYGENS

The *Cassini-Huygens* probe had two parts. *Cassini* is an orbiter. It orbits Saturn. *Huygens* is a lander. It separated from *Cassini*. *Huygens* landed on Titan. Titan is one of Saturn's moons.

VENERA

The Soviet Union sent many landers to Venus. They sent Venera 7 in 1970. It was the first to land on Venus. They sent Venera 9 in 1975. It took the first pictures from Venus.

LUNAR ROVERS

LUNOKHOD 1 AND 2

Lunokhod 1 was the first rover to land on the moon. The Soviet Union sent it in 1970. They sent *Lunokhod 2* in 1973. The rovers studied the surface of the moon.

LUNAR ROVING VEHICLE

Lunar Roving Vehicles were like cars. Three Apollo **missions** took them to the moon. They helped the astronauts see more of the surface.

MARS ROVERS

THERE HAVE BEEN four successful rovers on Mars. They studied the planet's soil and air.

CURIOSITY (2012)

Curiosity is the largest rover on Mars. It is the size of a van! It is a cutting-edge science lab on wheels.

SOJOURNER (1997)

SPIRIT & OPPORTUNITY (2004)

19

DOCKED
SPACECRAFT

WORK AND
LIVING AREAS

RADIATORS

SOLAR PANELS

SPACE STATION

The ISS was put together in stages.

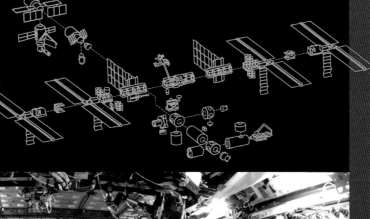

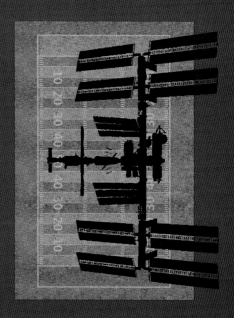

People from many countries have been to the ISS. Six people can be there at a time. They do science experiments. They also record what living in space is like.

FUTURE TRAVEL

Private companies will make space travel easier.

A person might walk on Mars.

We could get natural **resources** from asteroids.

In the future, space travel might become an everyday activity!

SPACE TRAVEL QUIZ

1. *Huygens* landed on what moon?

2. How many rovers have successfully made it to Mars?

3. The space shuttle is still being used today. **True or false?**

THINK ABOUT IT!
Which method of space travel would you pick and why?

GLOSSARY

comet – a mass of ice and dust that moves through space and develops a tail as it nears the sun.

gunpowder – a mixture of materials that explodes and is used in guns and cannons.

mission – a special job or assignment.

resource – something that is usable or valuable.

runway – a special road used for airplane takeoffs and landings.